Poems Prayers Testimonials Teachings

THE DEEP

Poems Prayers Testimonials Teachings

THE DEEP

WENDI CHALLENGER, REV. DR. JANET JENKINS STURDIVANT,
MICHELLE BROWN, ENID CHALLENGER, TAREEMA JEAN BAPTISTE,
KARLENE FRANCIS, REVEREND MARY ELLEN COLLIER, AUSTINA
MUI, MITSY-ANN ROBINSON-SIMMONDS, ERNESTEEN BROWN

ISBN: 978-1-4866-2614-4
eBook ISBN: 978-1-4866-2615-1

Word Alive Press
119 De Baets Street Winnipeg, MB R2J 3R9
www.wordalivepress.ca

Cataloguing in Publication information can be obtained from Library and Archives Canada.

This book is dedicated to its readers, and all its proceeds, after covering publishing expenses, will be directed towards funding affordable housing initiatives in Canada, the United States, and globally through ElLemuel. and other aligned organizations.

CONTENTS

PREFACE

> When He had stopped speaking, He said to Simon, "Launch out into the deep and let down your nets for a catch." (Luke 5:4, NKJV)

IN 2019, THE Holy Spirit impressed upon me the relevance of Luke 5:4, prompting the establishment of an intercessory prayer and study group we call Into the Deep. Out of the prayer and interaction of this group, as well as family and friends, The Deep was birthed. It has been a journey with many distractions along the way, but we have persevered.

Before delving into the details, let's revisit the events leading to this pivotal verse. Simon, James, and John were diligently cleaning their nets by the Lake of Gennesaret (the Sea of Galilee), seemingly oblivious to Jesus and the surrounding crowd. Having endured a night of unproductive fishing, they were away from their idle boats.

Jesus, however, observed their empty vessels and stepped into Simon's. Not only did He enter, He instructed Simon to *"put out a little from the land"* (Luke 5:3, NKJV) while He continued to teach the assembled crowd.

Following His discourse, Jesus urged Simon, *"Launch out into the deep and let down your nets for a catch"* (Luke 5:4, NKJV). Although initially hesitant, Simon, looking beyond the facts to the One instructing him, responded, *"Nevertheless at Your word I will let down the net"* (Luke 5:5, NKJV).

The Lord was calling me, just as He is calling all of us, to cultivate a deeper and enduring relationship with Him. May our response always echo Simon's words: "Nevertheless at Your word."

God not only seeks to reignite our passion for His Word; He also invites us to active obedience. As Proverbs 27:17 tells us, *"iron sharpens iron"* (NKJV), emphasizing our need for each other in our journey toward growth.

Into the Deep is a group of like-minded sisters in Christ. Our focus and desire is a deeper walk with the Lord in obedience and faith, igniting trust with the evidence of fruit.

Authentic transformation occurs in the deep, where we anchor our hope securely, according to Hebrews 6:19. In this profound space, we receive blessings, revelations, strength, vision, and boundless peace to share abundantly with others. It is in the deep that our desperate need for God is laid bare.

In *The Deep*, you will find a rich mix of scriptures, prayers, poems, teachings, and testimonials illustrating God's power and the experiences of women of faith. As you read this book, we hope you'll recognize your own journey and understand that what the Lord has done in our lives, He can and will do in yours. Remember that He *"is the same yesterday, today, and forever"* (Hebrews 13:8, NKJV).

God's Word is dynamic—it is life, a sword, breath, bread, water, and light. Join us as we embark on a journey to deepen our relationship with Christ. I pray that something extraordinary will begin to unfold within you as you engage with the scriptures contained herein. Whatever challenges you face, whatever experiences you have encountered, your answers lie in the Word. God knows your heart. Be blessed!

—Wendi Challenger

INTRODUCTION

FOR MOST OF us, life is filled with swift transitions. Since the COVID-19 pandemic, most of our lives have changed. What is important has changed. We focus now on family, goals, dreams unfulfilled, and our spiritual well-being. We have more questions than answers, yet we still seek to find the meaning of it all, whatever the *all* may be in our lives.

The title of this book is *The Deep*, because it goes deep into the experiences of each contributor and their spiritual experiences. The writings are a well of expressions and revelations brought about by situations and circumstances in each one's life. You will find truth and depth in the treasures of each word written on these pages. These contributors have shared the intimacy of each lesson learned by God and the hope that their journey will strengthen yours. *The Deep* is a collection of testimonies, stories, poems, and teachings to edify and remind you of the love God has for you no matter where you are or what you are experiencing right now.

Journey through *The Deep* and challenge yourself to meditate on the writings that speak to you specifically, the ones that speak your language or sit in your seat. Each contributor, without fail, loves the Lord and wants through their contribution for you to know you can take it. You can make it. Yes, you can! *The Deep* will strengthen your faith, renew your spirit, and increase your love for God. It will convince you that a life in God is worth living because better days are ahead.

—Rev. Dr. Janet Jenkins Sturdivant

PART ONE
POEMS

PERSONAL REFLECTIONS

THE EDGE
MICHELLE BROWN

So shall they fear the name of the Lord from the west, and his glory from the rising of the sun. When the enemy shall come in like a flood, the Spirit of the Lord shall lift up a standard against him. (Isaiah 59:19, KJV)

OUT OF THE depth of my desire, I long to be in Your will, but the weight of my past is with me still.

I'm reaching, wanting, hoping you will draw me in.

My life is at a standstill, with no will.

Wasting more time tosses me into a whirlwind.

My mind spins.

Here I go again, standing at the edge of possibility, waiting, wanting, reaching...

and then my hands stand still.

God, where are You? Everything around me is falling.

I grasp at pieces that I think will help me stop calling.

I put them together in hopes of a strong foundation,

Only to find that doing it myself makes it all go wrong.

The pieces scatter and go everywhere.

Then I'm back at the beginning, just standing there, at the edge.

The enemy wants to get us to the edge,

Where he feeds us lies to the point that we doubt God and all He has for us.

It's true, the burdens may feel overwhelming.

But remember, even in the face of adversity,

God promises to raise up a standard against the enemy when He comes in like a flood (Isaiah 59:19).

Take comfort in knowing that His Word will see you through.

Let it be your strength, your guide, and what you hold on to.

Prayer: Lord, help me to surrender all to You. I'm so tired of carrying it all. Holy Spirit, give me the strength to release it into the Master's hands and trust His plans. Amen.

GRATITUDE
KARLENE FRANCIS

Let them give thanks to the Lord for his
unfailing love and his wonderful deeds for
mankind. (Psalm 107:21)

GREAT ARE YOU, Lord, my God of grace.
To You this day I will sing Your praise
For Your goodness, kindness, and grace.
My heart is filled with gratitude.

The beauty of Your creative works
Fills my heart with peace and joy.
Your splendor in all the universe
Captivates my heart with thankfulness.
I will praise Your name.
My heart is filled with gratitude.

To You alone who sits on the throne,
Whose universe is Yours alone,
To guide my life throughout my days
And help me to follow all Your ways,
My heart is filled with gratitude.

I try to find the words to express
My appreciation for Your awesomeness.

My soul will sing of Your faithfulness
And remain in Your righteousness.
I praise the Lord that I am blessed.
My heart is filled with gratitude.

When I think of Your great name
And all the goodness it contains,
I bless You, adore You.
With thankfulness I praise Your name.
You are perfect in all Your ways.
My heart is filled with gratitude.

———————

Prayer: When I think of the goodness of Jesus and what He has done for me, my soul cries out, "Hallelujah! My God has set me free." Truly, Lord, I am grateful that I can call on You at any time of the day or night. Help me to remain grateful in every area of my life. I thank You for Your many blessings past, present and future, in Jesus's name, amen.

REJOICE IN THE DAY

KARLENE FRANCIS

> The Lord has done it this very day; let us rejoice
> today and be glad. (Psalm 118:24)

LORD, AS YOU bless us with another day, lead us so we do not go astray.

Let us never take the day for granted but use it in a positive way.

Guide our hearts to do what is right. Show us Your way and how to follow through.

If we are struggling throughout the day, please remind us, Lord, always to pray.

Though oftentimes we don't get it right, help us, Lord, never to lose insight.

Help us to rebuke the enemy when he draws near, for Your words are absolute and very clear.

I praise You, God, for the battle has been won, through the redemptive blood of Your dear Son.

Through this sacrifice, my soul has been set free so I can have life for all eternity.

THE BEAUTY I SEE
MITSY ANN SIMMONDS ROBINSON

THE BEAUTY OF God is everywhere I look.
So incredibly awesome,
it transcends the confines of a single book.
The smell of the sweet spring air hinted by showers of rain.
Sprouts of plant bursting from the earth
that once looked so plain.
I am struck by the colorful beauty of every flower.
I can admire all day, but each day does not have enough hours.
Just a short summer walk in the park and I am overwhelmed
by God's goodness.
The canopy of trees gives me shade from
the master star of brightness.
A great willow tree over a hundred years old
took my breath away.
It took the arms of my entire family to hug its massive old hand-
some trunk right away.
The animals are hoping, running, jumping,
flying, crawling, or hiding.
Hoping to catch the magnificent dainty butterfly, but the mos-
quitoes tried biting.
The harmonious singing of the birds is music to my ears.
Not to mention their beautiful colors: orange, blue, brown,
black, yellow, red, and some in pairs.
Their singing competes with the sound of the rushing river.

Oh my, I cannot believe the stillness of where two rivers meet,
now that's the winner.
Everything that God made is incredibly special and beautiful.
Including me and you, so for His goodness and love I am forever
grateful.

———————

Prayer: Dear heavenly Father, thank You so much for helping me see the beauty in everything You have created. Thank You for the sun, sky, air, plants, and animals that provide everything we need. Thank You for the majestic beauty of nature and the healing effect it has on my body and mind. Lord, please forgive me when I take Your creation for granted. My dear creator and Father, please continue to bless me with the abundant beauty and healing powers of Your creation. You are the marvelous one true God who takes care of my needs every day. You are worthy to be praised! Lord, I love You. take full control of my life, in the mighty name of Jesus, amen.

YOURS FOREVER
ENID CHALLENGER

For the Lord disciplines those he loves, and
he punishes each one he accepts as his child.
(Hebrews 12:6, NLT)

ABBA FATHER, I am Yours,
Yours forevermore,
Sought with the love of Jesus,
Bought by His blood.
My future is secure.

Chorus
I sing this sweet, sweet story
Of the Christ who died for me.
With His precious blood He saved me,
On the cross of Calvary.

Nothing is hidden from God's sight;
He sees and knows all things.
His presence is always with me,
Oh! What awesome peace it brings.

I cannot do without You
Oh Savior of the lost.

Life without You would be useless,
Thank God, I have counted the cost.

You hold me responsible for my life,
My behavior, attitude, and actions,
My accountability would be without merit.
Praise God for the help of the Holy Spirit.

With the rod of correction
God's love is shown;
It proves that I am His child
His chastisement is His protection,
It conforms me to the likeness of Christ.

Holy Spirit, my counsellor and guide,
Stay close beside me whatever betide.
Your omnipotent, omnipresence perfect love for me.
Empowers, instructs, and directs a path
Only spiritual eyes can see.

GOD'S UNCONDITIONAL LOVE
ENID CHALLENGER

> For Christ's love compels us, because we are
> convinced that one died for all, and therefore
> all died. (2 Corinthians 5:14)

YOU LOVE ME like no other can
So unconditionally.
Lord Jesus, You love me,
A broken vessel,
For all eternity.

Your love had captivated me,
A sinful soul on bended knee.
Thank God for the blood on Calvary shed;
It was to the cross where I was led.

Your nail-pierced body bled for me,
Hung starkly upon the cruel tree.
Yes, I was there, let it be told;
For me You suffered and died alone.

Who am I that You should care?
For an unworthy child in despair?
What is my mission, my fate, my task?
My master builder, my Savior, my mark.

Hallelujah! What a Savior.

Hallelujah to Christ the King.

Children of God's creation,

Purchased by redemption,

Come, raise your voices and joyfully sing,

"Hosanna to our Lord and King."

Come, raise your voices and joyfully sing,

"Hosanna, hosanna, to Christ the King."

GOD SEES AND KNOWS ALL THINGS
ENID CHALLENGER

ON THE MORNING of May 13, 2003, during my daily devotional, I felt spiritually inspired to write this poem based of the book of Hebrews 4. It is my hope that this poem will inspire, bless, encourage, and challenge you.

God understands our every need.
He knows our every fear.
With caring hands, He gently leads
And wipes away our every tear.

Our wounded spirits He does mend
With loving and inspiring words
That fill our bosoms and pierce our hearts,
More than the sharpest part of a two-edged sword.

None is hidden from His sight
For we are His creation.
With tender love He molds and shapes
Our lives into perfection.

All things are naked to His eyes.
He hears and knows all things.
With our weaknesses He does sympathize;
He is our God, our Father and King.

With grateful hearts we do give thanks
For His unlimited grace and love,
For all the blessing He bestows
Upon us from above.

Thanks be to Thee, Christ Jesus,
For Your blood on Calvary shed
To redeem us from the enemy
And restore us from the dead.

DEDICATED TO THE BRIDE AND GROOM
ENID CHALLENGER

THE ORGAN IS playing.
Oh! Hear the people singing.
The day of your wedding has come
And you have now made your vow.

To love and to cherish in good times and bad,
You both have agreed to share all your griefs in sad times
For richer, for poorer, in sickness and health,
May God help you keep these promises at length.

With your hearts and hands, now unite
In bonds of love to hold you tight.
May all your hopes and dreams come true
And bind you ever closer anew.

Let God be your strength, your guide and stay,
And love be your passion for each other each day.
That your children may grow and learn from you.
That love is lovelier when shared by two.

EMOTIONAL JOURNEYS

SEE HER

MICHELLE BROWN

She will do him good and not evil all the days
of her life. (Proverbs 31:12, KJV)

THERE IS AN image of her that you have decided to believe, but
that is not the truth of who she is.
See her for who God created her to be.
See her as the wife you called from above.
See her as God's covering love.
See her as strength by your side.
See her as your partner in life
to build a home without stress or strife.
See her as her heart unfolds, drawing you in to loosen strongholds.
See her as your ally in battle, together forging a stronger front,
with no need to keep anything hidden.
See her as your eternal companion in this lifetime.
See her as your darling wife.

A PRAYER FOR HUSBANDS
MICHELLE BROWN

HUSBANDS, I PRAY that God would give you a revelation of truth, the truth of who you are in Him. I pray that He would open your eyes to your worth and purpose, that you would see value in your life and hope to accomplish all that He has for you. Let the revelation of His Word become real to you so you can pursue it with passion. I pray that you would be free from your past and press on to a future that is full of God's grace and mercy. God is waiting on you. Do not be afraid. Release it all to Him.

A NOTE TO A HUSBAND
MICHELLE BROWN

> The Lord shall fight for you, and he shall hold
> your peace. (Exodus 14:14, KJV)

BEFORE GOD AND man, we committed to each other.
To have and to hold, for better or worse, in sickness and in health,
till death do us part.
Those are the words that echoed from our hearts.
Let us never stop believing, trying, and hoping.
Let us build and rely on each other.
We can never go far beyond repair.
God's hand is always on our marriage; He is always there.
Do not doubt what He can do, because I know for sure
 He can make our marriage forever new.
God knows our hearts; there is still a battle to fight.
Our marriage is sacred and holy in His sight.
He is ready for battle with sword drawn high.
We stand behind Him with heads lifted high.
The fight is His to win, His Word says so.
There is no battle too hard.
We just have to let go.
We press on as He goes before us, cutting down the enemy's plan because He has so much more.
He plans not to harm but to give us hope and a future.

So let us continue and press on each day.
As we hide His words in our hearts, He will guide the way.
Together we stand with victory on our lips, praising Him for being with us in this.

––––––––––

Prayer: Lord, I express gratitude for Your presence in every marriage. May partners remain accountable to one another, establishing an unbreakable foundation of trust amid uncertainties. Strengthen their bond by drawing them closer to You. Allow them to acknowledge their dependence on Your guidance for a marriage that aligns with Your will. In Jesus's name, amen.

A PRIDEFUL HEART
KARLENE FRANCIS

Pride goes before destruction, and a haughty
spirit before a fall. (Proverbs 16:18, NKJV)

PRIDE MAKES YOU arrogant and deceives you into thinking
you are good.
You don't see the need to be corrected
and wonder why you should
when in your eyes you are doing good.
Pride makes you think you are so smart when all it does
is ruin your heart.
Pride does not promote you;
instead, it destroys and isolates you.
It causes you to become puffed up, believing that you haven't
committed any sin, when all it is doing is destroying you.
Pride harbors grudges, envy, and lies
and causes insecurity within.
Pride ravages the soul; it hardens the heart and makes you
become cold.
Pride is a weakness, so don't confuse it for strength.
So, give it up and repent.
Humility is best when you put pride to rest.
So cast down your pride and with God you will abide.
Don't let pride destroy your soul, because God's beauty
you will not behold.

He does not delight in the prideful heart; from you His grace will depart.

> A man's pride shall bring him low, but humble in spirit will retain honor. (Proverbs 29:23, NKJV)

———

Prayer: Lord, as we search our hearts today, help us to remove the spirit of pride that may rise within us. Create in us clean and pure hearts. Give us a Christ-like nature so we can care for others as we would care for ourselves. Teach us to show kindness and humility in our everyday walk with You and help us to humble ourselves in all that we do. In Jesus's name we pray, amen.

PART TWO
PRAYERS

PERSONAL CONVERSATIONS

HEALTHY HEART
TAREEMA JEAN BAPTISTE

Create in me a clean heart, O God; and renew a right spirit within me. (Psalm 51:10, KJV)

And the Lord answered me, and said, Write the vision, and make it plain upon tables, that he may run that readeth it. For the vision is yet for an appointed time, but at the end it shall speak, and not lie: though it tarry, wait for it; because it will surely come, it will not tarry. (Habakkuk 2:2–3, KJV)

I WROTE THIS prayer when my husband and I were going through premarital counselling. To give you some context, the pastor who married us purposely pushed us emotionally and spiritually.

His reasoning, first, was that if he could break us up, it would be easy for the devil to do it. Second, he wanted to get us to a raw and naked place before God to allow for true change as God rebuilt us together.

This was a powerful spiritual experience that really bonded us. I share the prayer I wrote to God after the most intense counselling session. In that session, I realized that I was walking around with a very unhealthy heart. I realized that I was carrying so much emotional baggage, and if something didn't change I would carry it all into my marriage.

My hope is that sharing this prayer will inspire you to be raw and naked before God and allow Him to renew in you a clean and healthy heart.

––––––––––

Dear God,

You said in Your Word that we should write the vision and make it plain. So here I go. My vision for my marriage is to have a Godly marriage. I know that statement is broad, but God, You are broad. You are everything, everywhere, and in all the details. Lord, I want and need what You have for my marriage. I want to be like the wife in Proverbs 31.

Lord, give me a new heart. Please take away my broken heart. Take away the sadness, the loneliness, and the bitterness. Please take away the heaviness, the hurt, the rejection, and the unforgiveness. Please take away the self-hate, the self-loathing, and the self-pity. Please take away the sorrow, the pain, and the shame. Take it away! I am tired of it. I don't want it anymore. No more!

Oh God, give me a new heart directly from You. Give me a healthy heart, pure and clean. Give me a heart that feels peace, love, and joy at all times. Give me a heart that is saturated in love. No matter what is going on, I will always feel love. I want love from You, God, first—unshakable, steadfast, strong, never-ending, warm, and true.

Through You, God, I want love from my husband that is honest, faithful, unconditional, and outpouring. I want my heart to overflow with joy, hope, and optimism. I want my heart to be happy and shine. I want my heart to love itself and love me.

Please, Lord, I want my heart to be humble and forgiving. I want my heart to breathe without regrets or shackles. Please let my heart be free and content. God, give me a new heart from You that dwells in You always, Amen.

OVERALL DAILY PRAYER
TAREEMA JEAN BAPTISTE

FATHER, IN THE name of Jesus we thank You for Your wisdom, guidance, and peace bestowed upon us. We stand unified in faith, trusting in Your Word and declaring that this year we will be successful, in the name of Jesus.

We thank You that no weapon formed against us shall prosper. We thank You that we will stay COVID-free, flu-free, bacteria-free, lice-free, and disease-free. You are Jehovah Rapha, our healer! We thank You for the hedge of protection around us. We charge our angel army to encamp around our entire community and family 24/7 like a mighty phalanx.

We know that all things work together for good, because we are called as Christian warriors to advance Your Kingdom, and You will provide what we need. We declare there are no limits for our ministry or business. We thank You for the blessings from heaven that rain upon our community and family every day.

We know that You are Jehovah Jireh, our provider. We stand in expectant faith for miracles of provision for everything we need.

Jehovah Nissi, our King, we ask that You reign freely over our community and family. We surrender to Your discernment and guidance. We thank You in advance for showing us how to uniquely educate, nurture, and develop each child in our community and family. As we communicate with each other, we ask that we do so with the love and grace of Christ. We declare that all communication will be clear and productive, bearing fruit of healthy relationships and Kingdom favor to help expand Your vision for our community and family.

Lord, our righteous redeemer, help us to stand firm in our faith. Help us to be beacons of righteousness within our community. Keep us humble and pure of heart. Keep in us joy, peace, patience, kindness, generosity, faithfulness, gentleness, self-control, and most of all love, as we are servants in Your name. We pray that in all we do we represent the unconditional love, mercy, and grace You have for all people. We declare that our community and family will be an example of Christ's love for all.

Jehovah Shalom, we rest in Your peace that passes all understanding, confident that Your Word is true and will not return to us void. We remain hopeful that Your vision will prevail. We declare that our community and family belong to the almighty God. We confess that all this shall be done, in Jesus's name, amen.

SALVATION PRAYER
WENDI CHALLENGER

> For it is by grace you have been saved, through
> faith—and this is not from yourselves, it is the
> gift of God—not by works, so that no one can
> boast. (Ephesians 2:8–9)

DEAR LORD JESUS,

I come before You with a grateful heart, acknowledging the sacrifice You made on the cross for my sins. I recognize that I am in need of Your forgiveness and salvation.

I confess my sins and shortcomings, and I ask for Your mercy. Thank You for offering me the free gift of salvation through Your death and resurrection.

I believe in You, Jesus, as my Savior and Lord. I receive Your forgiveness and invite You into my life to guide and transform me. I surrender my will to Yours and choose to follow You.

Thank You for Your love, grace, and the promise of eternal life. May Your Holy Spirit dwell within me, empowering me to live a life that honors You.

In Your precious name I pray, amen.

INTERCESSORY PRAYERS

PRAYER FOR YOUTH
ERNESTEEN BROWN

HEAVENLY FATHER, I come before You at this time with a burden on my heart for youths. Lord, I give You praise, honor, and glory for You alone are worthy to be praised. Lord, I pray that You would fortify and strengthen youth in the Kingdom and help them to be grounded firmly and deeply in you. I pray that they would not be shaken when times get hard but that they will know without a shadow of a doubt who to turn to. Help them to know that You are near. And when the enemy comes upon them like a flood, lift up a standard against him and find a way of escape for them. Show them Your power, Lord. Show them Your glory. Keep their eyes and hearts focused on You.

Lord, let me not overlook the youth who haven't found salvation. I bring them before Your throne and ask that You draw them close, changing their hearts from stone to flesh, so Your words can deeply impact them. Our sons and daughters are among them, and so we come in Your name, Jesus. We know in whom we believe, and we know that nothing is impossible for You to do. As we raise them in prayer, we ask for the fulfillment of the desires of our hearts. We know it is not Your will that any should perish but that all would come to know You. Our youth are the future, and we want them to know that our prayers are with them, with the assurance that You will answer on their behalf. You called them to come because they are strong. Let no one despise their youth. Help them to find their way to You.

Lord, You are the Great I Am, the great High Priest, King of Kings, and Lord of Lords. I want to thank You for the lives You will transform through Your power. You know them by name, their nature, their hearts, their location, and the plans You have for their lives. Make their hearts ready to receive the seed of Your life-transforming Word. Cleanse them from all unrighteousness in Jesus's name with thanksgiving, Amen.

PRAYER FOR THE SICK
ERNESTEEN BROWN

HEAVENLY FATHER, AS I enter Your throne room I lift Your name above every other name. I give You all my praise, worship, and honor. Your Word tells us that we are to confess to one another and pray for one another that we may be healed (James 5:16).

Today I am praying for the sick and ask that You would lay Your hands on them so they may recover. Because You are a God who heals, I come to You now, the author and finisher of our faith. Lord, the enemy is bombarding my mind and disturbing my peace with illness. I know that sickness does not come from You, and I also know that You have given me the authority and power to lay hands on the sick and they shall recover. Help me walk in that faith, applying faith to the promises. Remind me that nothing is impossible with You. There is no sickness, disease, or pain You cannot cure. Lord, I take a stand and rebuke every plan of the enemy in Jesus's name. I stand on the Word of God. Healing is *"the children's bread"* (Matthew 15:26). I praise You because You honor Your Word above Your name.

Help me to walk in the truth of Your Word, Lord, in order to stop the enemy in his tracks. Help me to resist him so he flees. The enemy comes to steal, kill, and destroy. He does not love us; sickness is one of the ways in which he attempts to distract us. I know whom I trust. God, You are almighty and all-powerful. You do all things well. Lord, send Your Word, restore my body today, and touch my mind and soul. Thank You, Lord, for the healing that is on the way. Amen.

PRAYER FOR THE HOMELESS
WENDI CHALLENGER

What good is it, my brothers and sisters, if someone claims to have faith but has no deeds? Can such faith save them? Suppose a brother or a sister is without clothes and daily food. If one of you says to them, "Go in peace; keep warm and well fed," but does nothing about their physical needs, what good is it? (James 2:14–16)

GRACIOUS AND COMPASSIONATE Father, we come before You with heavy hearts, lifting up those who are homeless and marginalized in our communities. You are a God of mercy and compassion. We ask for Your loving presence to surround those who find themselves without a place to call home.

Lord, we pray for those who sleep on the streets, in shelters, or in temporary conditions. Comfort them in their struggles, provide for their needs, and grant them the strength to endure challenging circumstances.

May Your grace be upon those who feel invisible, rejected, and forgotten. Open our hearts to see them as You see them, with love and dignity. Move us to extend a helping hand, to advocate for their rights, and to work towards solutions that address the root causes of homelessness.

Lord, we also lift up those who serve in shelters, outreach programs, and support services. Grant them wisdom, compassion, and resources to make a positive impact on the lives of the homeless.

In Your mercy, Lord, bring an end to homelessness. Inspire communities to come together in solidarity, compassion, and understanding. May we all play a part in creating a world where everyone has a safe and secure place to call home.

We entrust the homeless into Your loving care, knowing that You are the God of hope and restoration. In Jesus's name we pray, amen.

PART THREE
TESTIMONIALS

STORIES OF TRANSFORMATION

CHARGE OVER ME
WENDI CHALLENGER

For He will give His angels charge concerning you, to guard you in all your ways. (Psalm 91:11, NASB)[1]

AFTER DROPPING MY daughter off at university to kickstart her postsecondary journey, I pitched in to organize her dorm room before heading back home. The prior night's preparations for the four-hour drive to campus had left me a bit tired.

Despite my fatigue, I decided to head back home. My daughter, understanding my state, put forth several convincing reasons to dissuade me from driving. While I acknowledged her concerns, my primary desire was to get a good night's sleep in my own bed after such a long day.

In the end, she yielded to my unwavering insistence, opting for the next best thing: she prayed for God's protection over me.

Once in the car and settled, I also prayed for God's traveling mercy before driving off. There was no doubt in my mind that I would make it home safely. After all, though my body was tired, I was fully awake.

---

[1] The Hebrew word translated here as *charge* refers to a directive or command, or even an instruction for the protection of one who trusts in God. I can also refer to a divine command. Put simply, this means that God will specifically instruct His angels to protect and watch over us.

Knowing that munching keeps me alert, I generally have snacks when driving long distances. This occasion was no different and I began munching on dried fruit.

As the snacks dwindled, though, so did my energy. I turned up the sermon playing on the radio to stay alert. Realizing that I needed a bit more pep, I decided to call a friend.

The phone rang three times and an exhausted voice spoke slowly into my ear. "Hello?"

"Oh my goodness," I replied. "You sound pooped."

She confirmed her own tiredness and inquired about my day. I explained that I was heading home but experiencing a drop in energy, hence the reason for the call. I told her to go to bed, but she refused and insisted on keeping me company until I arrived home safely.

My friend became energized and the conversation was uplifting and rejuvenating. However, it lasted no more than a half-hour because my phone decided to drop the call. Imagine my annoyance! I frantically tried to reconnect, but nothing worked. I kept trying until my phone died.

Here I was, in the dead of night, blackness all around me, on a two-lane highway in the middle of the country. The only lights illuminating the street were the high beams of the vehicle driving towards me.

Still a few hours from home, it was just me, God, the pastor on the radio, and my GPS. No snacks and no immediate way to regain communication, since my old cell would take some time to recharge.

I learned later that my friend was feverishly trying to regain the connection as well. But having no other recourse, she prayed.

It turns out that my mother was also trying to reach me to no avail and resorted to prayer as well. Prayer changes things!

I prayed once more for God's protection and turned up the radio.

I would be lying if I told you that I remember falling asleep. All I remember is listening to a sermon... prior to waking up with my hand gripped on the steering wheel as I barreled down someone's driveway poised to ram into the back of their car.

Slamming on the brake with all my might, I came to a screeching halt, just centimeters from the parked car.

There was dead silence. No one moved inside the house, and nothing moved outside. And instantaneously I recognized who had awoken me in the nick of time to stop the car.

Needless to say, I sat there in shock. In this state of astonishment and reverence, I praised God and expressed gratitude for His grace and mercy. I acknowledged that He had assigned His angel to watch—take charge—over me.

Regaining my composure, I began to back out of the driveway. It took longer than I thought because shrubs lined both sides. To avoid damaging my car, I needed five tries to maneuver my way out of there. I had managed to drive in a straight line while asleep yet had difficulty reversing while fully awake!

You see, when God takes the wheel, the car drives straight and sure. But the struggle becomes real when we take the helm. God is amazing!

I finally reached the end of the driveway with still not a hint of movement from my serene surroundings, not even the rustle of a mouse.

I expected to turn onto the highway, since that's where I last remembered driving. Instead the GPS directed me to make a right turn and proceed to the end of the road. Once there, it instructed me to turn left and continue again. After following this guidance, I at last turned right onto the highway I recalled driving along.

Did you catch that? My heavenly Father had guided me from

DID YOU CATCH THAT?

the dark highway to a lit driveway in a small country town, where He woke me up to stop the car. He spared my life twice in one night. What a mighty God we serve!

To add even more amazement to this experience, the house I was led to was the only one with its driveway light turned on. Keep in mind that the highway and community were completely dark except for my high beams, that fateful driveway light, and the porchlight of a house at the corner where the GPS instructed me to make the left turn. All glory to God!

Needless to say, I remained completely alert for the rest of the journey. I reached home safely, gratitude filling my heart. The awareness of my Father's love triumphed over any fear of deviating from his vision and purpose for my life.

Never allow anyone to convince you that anything is beyond God's capability, not even your own mind.

> With man this is impossible, but with God all
> things are possible. (Matthew 19:26)

> God is our refuge and strength, an ever-present
> help in trouble. (Psalm 46:1)

Let's persist in placing our trust in Him. His ways are *"past finding out"* (Romans 11:33, KJV). Praise be to God!

———

Prayer: Father, I love You. I acknowledge Your faithfulness, provision, protection, grace, mercy and love for me. I will not neglect to honor and adore You. Thank You for being my protector and giving Your angels charge over me. Continue to gird me with Your hedge of protection. I depend on You and exalt You today. You are worthy to be praised. I lift holy hands right now to You, the King of Kings and Lord of Lords, knowing that nothing can separate me from Your love, the author and finisher of my faith. In the name of Jesus I pray, amen!

GOD'S ESTEEM
WENDI CHALLENGER

> I praise you because I am fearfully and
> wonderfully made; your works are wonderful, I
> know that full well. (Psalm 139:14)

I SEE MYSELF as a leader, not someone who follows. To my knowledge, I never followed the crowd. I resisted peer pressure, even when I was urged to drink in my undergraduate years.

I have my fears and shortcomings, of course. I am not a perfect woman, although I am progressing in the Lord.

However, I never would have thought that I had low self-esteem. My walk, talk, and demeanor never revealed it. I suppose avoiding photographs should have been a sign, but it wasn't. Only when the Lord unveiled the truth and revealed the source of my low self-esteem did I become aware of it.

You see, after an unsuccessful marriage, I asked the Lord to reveal the underlying issue. In a still, soft voice, He spoke self-esteem into my spirit. I was surprised and deliberated on the voice's validity. I never would have imagined that I had this issue.

God then directed me to Psalm 139:14 to school me on His esteem. I was familiar with the passage. In fact, I had quoted it on a number of occasions.

I was dumbfounded and actually said, "Father, that can't be true." Can you imagine?

He revealed the source of my low self-esteem by taking me to an incident in my childhood when I had been called a name, and another incident that occurred in high school. I hadn't realized that these two incidents had made an impact on me.

Words are powerful! I set out to study and implement the truth of Psalm 139:14 in my life. I learned that the power of man's words is eradicated by the power of God's Word.

I dug into the meaning of Psalm 139:14.

"I praise you..." God's greatness and might make Him deserving of our praise. As we marvel at His awesome power, we spark a commitment to follow and obey Him.

"I am fearfully made..." The Hebrew term *yare*, referring to the fear of the Lord, doesn't suggest terror. Instead it emphasizes deep reverence and respect. God doesn't want us to cower in fear or anxiously look over our shoulders; He is not a villain but a Savior.

"I am wonderfully made..." The Hebrew word *pala* refers to something unique, separate, or distinguished. In layman's terms, it means that God made us special.

"Your works are wonderful..." Everything God creates is very good, according to Genesis 1:31. We are all God's masterpieces, whether it's you, me, your cousin, your aunt, the person experiencing homelessness, or the physically disabled person nearby.

Consider this: there are around seven billion people on the earth, and counting, yet each person's fingerprint is distinct. Reflect on the fact that no one else has your fingerprint or retina scan. You are truly unique, one of a kind, and special!

"I know that full well." We know our worth because the Word of God tells us. God is our creator and we have been made in His

55

image. You see, it's God who created your innermost being and knitted you together in your mother's womb. You are an original design.

In summary, David praises God by acknowledging the incredible way in which God created him. Similarly, you should express gratitude to the Lord for how uniquely He made you. You are more precious than the largest diamond ever found, which by the way weighs 530 carats.

YOU ARE NOT JUST RARE, YOU ARE BEYOND RARE. YOU ARE THE ONLY ONE OF YOU IN EXISTENCE AND THERE WILL NEVER BE A DUPLICATE.

Scratch that. You are not just rare, you are *beyond* rare. You are the only one of you in existence and there will never be a duplicate. Your fingerprints are exclusively yours.

If you ever doubt your value, I hope you now recognize and embrace your worth in God. Regardless of your background, relationships, or origins, remember that you are *"fearfully and wonderfully made."* Claim your God-given esteem!

———

Prayer: Father, I praise You because You have a plan and a purpose for my life. You took the time to knit me together in my mother's womb. I am grateful for how amazing You made me. I recognize that my body is a temple and understand that I have to take care of it. I now take captive every criticizing thought I have about myself and speak the truth of Your Word over my life. I receive the truth that I am Your masterpiece because I know that You do not make mistakes. I am made in Your image and likeness. There is only one me. I accept your esteem and resonate with divine approval. Thank You for Your love and guidance through the Holy Spirit. In Jesus's name, amen.

TRUSTING GOD
WENDI CHALLENGER

> Let us not become weary in doing good, for at
> the proper time we will reap a harvest if we do
> not give up. (Galatians 6:9)

MY GRANDMOTHER PASSED away while I was in graduate school. With no extra funds at my disposal, I didn't see how I would be able to attend her funeral.

I called my mother to share the bad news. My mother instantaneously began to pray that God would provide and assured me that He would.

Soon after getting off the phone, I began to pray. I just had a quick conversation with the Lord. With confidence that He would make a way, I said, "Lord, I don't have the funds, but I do have a credit card. I'm going to trust You to provide the funds to pay it off when I return." You see, I had a credit card for emergency purposes that I didn't use due to past experience.

I called a cousin of mine who had a friend who was a travel agent. Contacting the travel agent, I paid for my flight via the phone with credit. The agent even confirmed my credit card number before processing my payment.

My ticket arrived promptly after that, and I went to the funeral.

Upon my return to school, I anxiously anticipated the arrival of my credit statement. The statement came, yet the expense of my ticket wasn't listed. I called the credit card company and was told that it should show up on my next statement.

When the bill for the following month arrived, still there was no charge. That's when I realized that God had intervened.

Even now I find myself astonished. To this day, I have never been billed for the trip I took to my grandmother's funeral. God's ways are truly beyond comprehension and He answers prayers.

If you are trusting God for a request, know that James 4:3 assures us He will provide, as long as our intentions are not self-indulgent but align with His purpose. He can and will do it for you.

———————

Prayer: You are a wonderful, powerful, mighty, and omnipotent God. I am so glad that Your ways are not my ways, nor Your thoughts like mine. I trust You to answer every prayer of my heart that is in line with Your will and the truth of Your Word. Your greatness leaves me speechless and Your love fills me with confidence. Hallowed be Thy name. Grant me grace to trust You more. In Jesus's name, amen.

IF YOU ARE TRUSTING GOD FOR A REQUEST, KNOW THAT JAMES 4:3 ASSURES US HE WILL PROVIDE, AS LONG AS OUR INTENTIONS ARE NOT SELF-INDULGENT BUT ALIGN WITH HIS PURPOSE.

FRUIT-BEARING LESSONS
REV. MARY ELLEN COLLIER

> She speaks with wisdom, and faithful instruction
> is on her tongue. (Proverbs 31:26)

DUE TO HIS grace, kindness, and mercy, I have been abundantly blessed by the Lord. I have two amazing adult children, including my daughter and her husband, whom I consider my bonus son, and my son and his wife, whom I see as my bonus daughter. I also have four beautiful and intelligent grandchildren. While they may occasionally push boundaries more than their parents did, they possess the wisdom to recognize when it's time to refrain from such behavior.

Throughout my educational journey, I have earned two master's degrees, one in education and the other in divinity.

While these achievements are significant blessings, the two most valuable lessons I ever learned were imparted to me by my mother, Lillie, who completed her education up to the eleventh grade in a public school:

1. Every person must have their very own personal relationship and fellowship with Jesus.
2. Only what you do for Christ will last.

There are two scriptures that especially speak of knowing the Lord and having a personal relationship and fellowship with Him: Genesis 5:21–24 and 1 Samuel 17:37.

1. EVERY PERSON MUST HAVE THEIR VERY OWN PERSONAL RELATIONSHIP AND FELLOWSHIP WITH JESUS.

2. ONLY WHAT YOU DO FOR CHRIST WILL LAST.

The first talks about Enoch, who walked faithfully with God for more than three hundred years.

The second talks about David, who had a personal relationship and fellowship with the Lord at a very young age while caring for sheep. The Lord delivered David from the paw of the lion and the paw of the bear.

Then there's John 4, which tells the familiar story of the Samaritan woman who encountered Jesus at a well. There is so much to learn from this text, but I want to draw out two major points.

First, she didn't know Jesus. She asked whether He was a prophet and didn't realize that she was talking to the Son of God, the Savior of the world. She simply didn't know our Lord and Savior Jesus Christ.

Second, she confused the places we are to go for worship and the One whom we are to worship. Many people run around attending church programs for fellowship without knowing Jesus. I know because I was one of those people.

After this woman's encounter with Jesus, she went back to her town proclaiming the gospel of Jesus Christ.

Thanks be to God for these blessings.

PART FOUR
TEACHINGS

DAILY SPIRITUAL PRACTICES

A WOMAN HAS TO DO WHAT
A WOMAN HAS TO DO

REV. DR. JANET JENKINS STURDIVANT

Go, gather together all the Jews who are in Susa, and fast for me. Do not eat or drink for three days, night or day. I and my attendants will fast as you do. When this is done, I will go to the king, even though it is against the law. And if I perish, I perish. (Esther 4:16)

I WAS ELEVEN when my father passed and my stepmother, better known as my mother, was left alone to raise me and my brother. There were times when she sacrificed things she wanted and needed in order for us to get what we needed. We neither lacked nor wanted for anything. We lived well for a family in the city because my mother was a woman who did what she had to do to make life work for us.

My mother's life mirrored Esther's. Like Esther, she was backed up against the wall and came out fighting. Esther had been chosen by God to save His people. She didn't know this right away; she just thought she was the new queen.

However, God had other plans, as He often does!

It became clear that her people needed her to intercede on their behalf, and she would have to break protocol in order to do it.

At first Esther was very apprehensive. But Mordecai challenged her thoughts and her purpose. He wondered about God's purpose and plan for her. He even asked whether she had been put in the king's palace for such a time as this.

She gathered her thoughts and nerves and moved forward with what she knew had to be done. She covered herself in prayer and fasting. With the help of others, she went ahead and accomplished her God-given assignment.

"And if I perish, I perish," she said. "But I am going to see the king."

DO YOU HAVE AN ASSIGNMENT TODAY? IS IT CHALLENGING? TRUST GOD AND GO FORTH. HE PROMISED NEVER TO LEAVE OR FORSAKE US. YOU CAN DO IT!

This reminds us of our Lord and Savior Jesus. When He was on His way to His assignment at the cross of Calvary, He too hesitated for a moment. But He bowed to the will of the Father and did what he had to do in order to save humankind.

Let's remember Esther and Jesus and how they wrestled with their assignments.

Do you have an assignment today? Is it challenging? Trust God and go forth. He promised never to leave or forsake us. You can do it!

———

Prayer: Father, I believe. Help my unbelief. Give me the courage to fulfill my assignment no matter the obstacles or challenges that seem to be in my way. If You gave me the assignment, I trust You will help me to accomplish it. In Jesus's name I pray, amen.

THANKFUL IN ALL CIRCUMSTANCES
AUSTINA MUI

WITHOUT A DOUBT, we will all face trials and uncertainties in life. In these moments, it can be hard not to ask, "Why, God? Why did You let this happen to me?" These challenges cause us stress, anxiety, and sleepless nights. They make us feel scared, worried, and lost.

As I turn to scripture, I am continuously reminded that God loves us as His children, and He will always be with us. He is with us through times of joy and times of trials. We may not know or understand why God places us in different situations, but we must trust that God has His plans for us. Turn to God for strength and seek His will in times of trials and uncertainties.

GOD LOVES US AS HIS CHILDREN, AND HE WILL ALWAYS BE WITH US.

In 1 Thessalonians 5:16–18, we are reminded, *"Rejoice always, pray continually, give thanks in all circumstances; for this is God's will for you in Christ Jesus."* No matter the situation or outcome, I am encouraged to always give thanks to the Lord for all that He has done and continues to do in my life. Sometimes the answer might not be what we want or expect, but we must trust that God is our shepherd and will always lead us to what's best for us.

T—*"The Lord is my strength and my shield; my heart trusts in him, and he helps me; my heart leaps for joy, and with my song I praise him"* (Psalm 28:7).

H—*"Hallelujah! For our Lord God Almighty reigns"* (Revelation 19:6).

A—*"And the peace of God, which transcends all understanding, will guard your hearts and your minds in Christ Jesus"* (Philippians 4:7).

N—*"...neither height nor depth, nor anything else in all creation, will be able to separate us from the love of God that is in Christ Jesus our Lord"* (Romans 8:39).

K—*"Know that the Lord is God. It is he who made us, and we are his; we are his people, the sheep of his pasture"* (Psalm 100:3).

F—*"Fear not, for I am with you; be not dismayed, for I am your God; I will strengthen you, I will help you, I will uphold you with my righteous right hand"* (Isaiah 41:10, ESV).

U—*"....unto us a Child is born, unto us a Son is given; and the government will be upon His shoulder. And His name will be called Wonderful, Counselor, Mighty God, Everlasting Father, Prince of Peace"* (Isaiah 9:6, NKJV).

L—*"Let them give thanks to the Lord for his unfailing love and his wonderful deeds for mankind"* (Psalm 107:21).

———————

Prayer: Dear heavenly Father, we come to You in prayer with a thankful heart. Thank You, Lord, for all that You've done in our lives. Oh Lord, please forgive us for those times when we've doubted Your power and plans for us. May You continue to lead us, and may we continue to stand firm in our faith, knowing that You will always be with us in all circumstances. In Jesus's precious name we pray, amen.

WHEN GOD RESTORES PEACE
REV. DR. JANET JENKINS STURDIVANT

I will drive away these armies from the north. I will send them into the parched wastelands. Those in the front will be driven into the Dead Sea, and those at the rear into the Mediterranean. The stench of their rotting bodies will rise over the land." Surely the LORD has done great things! Surely the Lord has done great things! Don't be afraid, O land, be glad now and rejoice, for the Lord has done great things! (Joel 2:20–21:2, NLT)

AS WE MEDITATE ON this passage, it becomes obvious that God's people experienced some difficult days. The land was swarming with locusts, a plague severe enough to leave the people terrified, immobile, and mentally distressed. How could they fight locusts? How would they destroy them? There were far too many locusts to exterminate or ignore.

But the Lord told the people not to worry, assuring them that He would remove them. The Lord would restore their peace by destroying all the locusts in front of them and any that were behind them.

I rejoice that we, too, can take comfort in these words:

> We are hard pressed on every side, but
> not crushed; perplexed, but not in despair;
> persecuted, but not abandoned; struck down,
> but not destroyed. (2 Corinthians 2:8–9)

The Lord is on our side. And like the children of Israel, He fights for us, restoring our peace and joy in the midst of trouble. For this we rejoice and are truly glad!

———————

Prayer: Father, in the name of Jesus help us to trust You when we can't trace You. And help us to rest in Your love and protection. We know that if trouble gets to us, it has to come through You first. So help us to wait patiently upon You and be of good courage, for You will surely strengthen our hearts. In Jesus's name, amen.

ON EMPTY

WENDI CHALLENGER

All scripture is given by inspiration of God, and is profitable for doctrine, for reproof, for correction, for instruction in righteousness... (2 Timothy 3:16, KJV)

ONE SUMMER DAY, I found myself in a predicament while taking my daughter to work. Despite having noticed that the car's fuel gauge was on empty before embarking on the journey, I optimistically believed there was enough gas to reach our destination. Time was crucial and I didn't want her to be late for her job, which was just ten minutes away. The plan was to drop her off and promptly refuel at the nearby gas station.

As we drove, the car's performance started to decline. Yet I pressed on, passing two gas stations, convinced that I could make it to my intended refueling point. I repeatedly told myself, "I can make it. Only five more minutes to go... three more minutes to go..."

My optimism proved unfounded. The car came to a halt just shy of the gas station I had intended to reach.

The same is true in our spiritual lives. Many of us believe we can sustain our Christian walk through church on Sundays, or through monthly prayer and Bible study. However, it's unsustainable to rely solely on these reserves, which leads to spiritual vulnerability and stagnation.

Regular communication with the Lord through prayer and consistent study of His Word is essential. This practice helps us to know God better, exposes and addresses sin in our lives, provides solutions to identified sins, and guides us in applying biblical truths practically.

Just as driving a car on a near-empty tank clouds our sense of its ability to complete the journey, neglecting spiritual nourishment weakens our capacity to change direction and live according to God's truth.

Let us commit to studying and understanding the Scriptures and ensuring continuous communication with the Lord (1 Thessalonians 5:17). By doing so, we avoid the risk of stalling just moments from our destination. May we persevere in our faith, finishing the race and ultimately receiving our crown (2 Timothy 4:7–8).

―――――――

Prayer: Lord, forgive us for our frequent conformity to the ways of this world. Forgive us for neglecting Your Word. We thank You for Your mercy and grace. We are grateful that there is no condemnation to those who have a relationship with You. Help us to be more consistent and intentional in our prayer and study lives. Thank You for showing us the hindrances and idols in our lives, anything that takes time away from our communicating with You. Thank You for sustaining and protecting us in our lack of understanding. Grant us wisdom and understanding in Kingdom principles as we dive deep into our relationship with You. In Jesus's name, amen.

LOVE IN ACTION

MITSY ANN SIMMONDS ROBINSON

Greater love has no one than this: to lay down
one's life for one's friends. (John 15:13)

ONE OF MY favorite church sisters is seventy-six years old, but you
would never believe it because of her strength and what she does
for God and others.

Whenever she babysat for me, she arrived at my home on
time without fail. She made dinner for her family before walking
the half-hour to my home, refusing a ride because she consid-
ered the walk her exercise. She took excellent care of my daughters, sometimes I think even better than myself!

She gave me important tips about my Christian journey and
life in general. She taught me how to prepare remedies with nat-
ural herbs and plants for good health and longevity. She cooks
at church and brings food to the less fortunate and shut-ins. She
gives little gifts to the kids and helps out in the children's ministry.
She sacrifices her time so others can be happy.

When she sees me and my family, she always says "I love you"
and gives us hugs. When someone loves you, they usually show
it. I don't have to guess that this woman truly loves me, because
she demonstrates love in action.

Though she loves well, however, it pales in comparison to the
love our heavenly Father lavishes on us daily. His is an everlasting
love that provides us with everything we need and blesses us in so

many ways. He made the ultimate sacrifice which proves His love for us. He sent His one and only Son to die on the cross to forgive us of our sins—past, present, and future.

———

Prayer: Dear heavenly Father, thank You for showing me Your love each and every day. Thank You for providing my every need and blessing me with some of my wants. Thank You most of all for sending Your Son to die on the cross so my sins could be forgiven. Thank You for Your grace and salvation. My creator and maker, I honor and praise You. Help me to live a life that exudes Your love. I desire to be Your hands and feet where You have planted me. Lord, I love You. Take full control of my life. In the mighty name of Jesus, amen.

STANDING
MICHELLE BROWN

> For he hath not despised nor abhorred the affliction of the afflicted; neither hath he hid his face from him; but when he cried unto him, he heard. (Psalm 22:24, KJV)

SOMETIMES IN MARRIAGE, you come to a place of discouragement, loneliness, and disappointment, questioning the decisions you've made together as husband and wife. Being in this place can make you feel like you've failed. You get so overwhelmed with your hurt and sense of loss that you can't see that God is working things out for your good. Everything seems wrong and none of your efforts feel like enough. Your mind is so clouded that you can't see past the hurt. Your internal voice appears to be the most pronounced. What you once thought was good becomes tainted by circumstances and dark thoughts.

All you can do is throw your hands up to God in surrender. With tears streaming down your face and a full heart, you cry out to Him. But God is able to wipe every tear from your eyes and replace discouragement with encouragement, loneliness with unity, and disappointment with fulfillment. You must trust the process!

Prayer: Lord, I release everything to You in Jesus's name. I stand at the edge of myself, head high, and hands lifted to You, my master and deliverer. I dare not look to the right or left; my focus is on You and what You have in store for my marriage. Lord, I know there is a plan, for Your Word cannot lie. You said that all I need to do is trust You, so here I am. Please hear my cry.

BE WISE: TAKE CARE OF YOUR SOUL
ENID CHALLENGER

> Like apples of gold in settings of silver is a
> ruling rightly given. Like an earring of gold or
> an ornament of fine gold is the rebuke of a wise
> judge to a listening ear. (Proverbs 25:11–12)

THE BOOK OF Proverbs offers practical advice about wisdom and discipline. According to Proverbs 1:2, the wisdom contained in this biblical text emphasizes the importance of recognizing God in every circumstance. This mindfulness contributes to our growth—spiritually, socially, emotionally, and physically. In moments of stumbling, we rise, restoring our balance and summoning the courage to persist. Wisdom serves as our crucial first step toward a joyful recovery from the consequences of poor choices, hurt, and pain.

In Proverbs 25:11–28, we read about the behaviors that wisdom develops in us, such as choosing appropriate words and timing, attentively considering sound advice, and expressing ourselves with gentleness, patience, and humility. The passage identifies and discourages negative behaviors such as gossip, lying, a lack of self-control, treachery, and other undesirable conduct.

As we journey through life and reflect on our relationship with Jesus Christ, we can ask ourselves these questions:

1. Am I following Jesus every day?
2. Am I trusting in Him or doubting Him when faced with attacks from the enemy or my own mind?
3. Am I mindful that too much of a good thing might be harmful?
4. Do I need a mental reset?
5. Am I wisely dividing the Word?

In challenging times, it's essential to turn to the Holy Spirit. As our comforter and guide, the Holy Spirit empowers us to overcome overwhelming and negative habits, prevailing over them consistently.

Here is an exercise we can try:

1. List three actions from Proverbs 25:11–28 that speak to you. Why do they speak to you?
2. How can you practice self-control in your life?
3. In what area of your life are you lacking wisdom?
4. Meditate on one scripture weekly and speak life into your current circumstance.
5. Capture God's blessing in your life by journalling as you walk in wisdom.
6. Express your gratitude to the Lord daily.
7. Get connected with a church or Bible study group.

Discipline is an action that brings instruction; it is not meant as a punishment for sin. As our heavenly Father, God uses discipline to grow and refine our character.

At times we may look at discipline as burdensome and cruel, but Proverbs teaches that a lack of self-control is destructive to our soul. When we cultivate wisdom, our soul is protected.

So be encouraged. Continue to care for your soul through the wisdom of God's Word.

————

Prayer: Almighty God, our heavenly Father, creator of all things, we praise and magnify Your name. There is no one like You in heaven or on earth. We thank You for Your mercies that are new every morning. We bless You for the abiding presence of Your Holy Spirit in our lives. You promise to never leave or forsake us. We are grateful for the shed blood of Jesus Christ our redeemer, Savior, and Lord who died to rescue and reconcile us sinners back to You.

Mighty God, you correct us when we stray. Grant us the wisdom to realize that Your discipline stems from love. Bless us with the wisdom to understand that we are not being punished. Instead, blessings await us. James 1:5 says, *"If any of you lacks wisdom, you should ask God, who gives generously to all without finding fault, and it will be given to you."*

We need Your wisdom, Father God. Open our hearts and minds to receive and obey Your instructions. Please continue to direct us in the way we should go. Shed light on the path ahead of us. Illuminate our sins for repentance and guide us in nurturing our souls. We ask for You to develop our God-given gifts and talents. Refine, refresh, and humble us along the way.

Father, for those who do not know Your Son Jesus Christ as their personal Lord and Savior, please lead them to the well of ever-living water. Cause them to drink freely so they will never thirst again. Your mercies we ask in Jesus's name, Amen.

THEMATIC TEACHINGS

THINGS!

REV. DR. JANET JENKINS STURDIVANT

> And we know that in all things God works for
> the good of those who love him, who have
> been called according to his purpose. (Romans
> 8:28)

TRAGEDIES ARE COMMONPLACE. Diseases are running rampant and people seem to be slipping away. The economy's down and people can't get enough pay. Things!

Folks without homes are living out in the streets. Some have drug habits they just can't beat. With muggers and robbers, no place seems to be safe. Things!

You do your best and often it doesn't seem to be enough. Tests keep coming, one right after the other. The joy of the Lord is your strength, but your strength is waning right about now. You give your last to help those in need, but often you get no thanks or sense of real appreciation in return. You're on the battlefield, but lately it feels like you don't have all the weapons needed to win the war. Things!

These things are complicating your testimony. They're affecting your faith walk.

What shall we say about these things? Whether you're a preacher, teacher, mission worker, evangelist, or someone reading this meditation, you must agree that these are times to trouble our souls. But what do we say?

Well, Paul suggests that we speak what we know—and what we know is that all these things work together for our good, for those who love the Lord. The best and worst of life, the most difficult times and moments of ease, all work for our good. They work because we love God, and God loves us. They work because we are called by God and called for His glory.

It may not feel like it today, and we may not be able to see the path, but rest assured that these things are working for our good.

Paul adds a word of encouragement that each of us can hold on to:

> No, in all these things we are more than conquerors through him who loved us. For I am convinced that neither death nor life, neither angels nor demons, neither the present nor the future, nor any powers, neither height nor depth, nor anything else in all creation, will be able to separate us from the love of God that is in Christ Jesus our Lord. (Romans 8:37–39)

So again, I ask: what do we say to these things? We say, "I've got the victory! Hallelujah!"

———————

Prayer: Father, as I come, I want to first thank You for being the author and finisher of my faith. I want to thank You for being omnipotent, omnipresent, omniscient, and from everlasting to everlasting. I want to thank You for holding me in Your hand so no one and nothing can pluck me out. Holy Spirit, help me not to be overwhelmed by the many things I face in my life today, and help me to affirm Your presence and power to see me through. All this I ask in the name of my risen Lord and Savior, Jesus the Christ, Amen.

THE WORK
MICHELLE BROWN

> And God is able to bless you abundantly, so
> that in all things at all times, having all that you
> need, you will abound in every good work. (2
> Corinthians 9:8)

THERE IS ABSOLUTELY no doubt that marriage requires work if it is to bear fruit. To thrive, both partners must be purposeful and determined to put the relationship first.

God sees marriage as a covenant—not only to each other, but to Him as well. This is why He expects us to dedicate ourselves to building each other up. He wants us to recognize our role and responsibilities both to our spouse and to Him.

All the effort, time, planning, words spoken, and actions done to grow your marriage will not be in vain. God promises that in all things and at all times you will abound in every good work.

Pastor Robert Hampshire writes,

> When God, who created us and knows
> us, created marriage, he created it for our
> enjoyment and to display the gospel. It is one
> of the countless ways that God expresses his
> grace and love to us.
>
> And because of that, a couple that is
> focused on God will naturally have a more

blessed marriage because they are bound together by the strong "three strands" that Solomon talks about in Ecclesiastes 4:12: The husband, the wife, and God.[2]

Prayer: Lord, I pray that the truth of marriage will resonate in our hearts and propel us to do the work necessary to become individuals worthy of this covenant blessing called marriage. Show us how to do the work and give us extended grace and patience with each other. Lord, take our marriage to deeper places in You. Let our marriage in time be a reflection of You so that Your will can be done and Your name glorified. Amen.

[2] Robert Hampshire, "What Does the Bible Say About Marriage?" *The 95.9 Fish*. Date of access: August 14, 2024 (https://thefishcolumbus.com/articles/family/marriage/what-is-the-biblical-definition-of-marriage).

PRAISE THE LORD
REV. DR. JANET JENKINS STURDIVANT

> Praise God in his sanctuary; praise him in his mighty heavens. Praise him for his acts of power; praise him for his surpassing greatness. Praise him with the sounding of the trumpet, praise him with the harp and lyre, praise him with timbrel and dancing, praise him with the strings and pipe, praise him with the clash of cymbals, praise him with resounding cymbals. Let everything that has breath praise the Lord. Praise the Lord. (Psalm 150:1–6)

WHAT IS PRAISE? It can be defined as an expression of warm approval or admiration. We can praise people for a job well done. We can praise our loved ones for their many accomplishments. We can praise an artist for their beautiful work or an entertainer for a great performance, the best we have ever seen.

However, Psalm 150:6 says, *"Let everything that has breath praise the Lord."*

There are seven ways to praise:

- Towdah: sacrifice of praise.
- Yadah: hands raised.
- Barak: quiet voice.
- Halal: soul rejoice.
- Zamar: instrumental song.

- Tehilah: sing along
- Shabach: shout for joy.

This passage from Psalm 150 also tells us a few things about praise, including the where, the why, the how, and the when.

Where? In His sanctuary and in His mighty heavens. Why? For His acts of power and surpassing greatness. How? With the sounding of the trumpet, with the harp and lyre, timbrel and dancing, strings and pipe, and the clash of cymbals.

So how about when? We read, *"Let everything that has breath praise the Lord."* When we don't have breath, we can't praise Him. When we do have breath, we praise Him. Every day when we wake up, praise the Lord. Every night when we go to bed, praise the Lord. Every minute, every second, we should be praising the Lord.

God is so good to us.

We were taught by our parents to thank others when they give us something. Well, let's thank God and praise Him for all He has done and continues to do. We cannot be silent witnesses. We have to open our mouths, clap our hands, pat our feet, wave our arms, or do whatever else we need to in order to praise the Lord. He alone is worthy of our praise—not just for what He has done, but for the fact of who He is: a strong tower to whom we run and are safe. He is a miracle worker, a promise keeper, a light in our darkness.

WE CANNOT BE SILENT WITNESSES.

We praise Him for saving, sanctifying, and filling us with the Holy Spirit. We praise Him for life, love, and laughter. We praise

Him in the morning, in the evening, and all through the night. Let everything that has breath praise the Lord!

Prayer: Father, forgive me for those times when I have seemed ungrateful for Your blessings. Forgive me for taking Your love and protection for granted. I am so thankful that You love and care for me. I am thankful that there is none like You. You are my best friend. I love You, Lord. Lord, teach me the different expressions of praise so I can praise You to the fullest. In Jesus's name I pray, amen.

JESUS IS MY JOY
MITSY ANN SIMMONDS ROBINSON

> ...the joy of the Lord is your strength. (Nehemiah 8:10)

WHENEVER I GO back home and visit my cousin, he seems more joyful than the last time I saw him. He tells me about all the problems he faces, but none of them seem to bother him. The more problems he has, the happier he seems to be. His joy is contagious and the hugs he gives last until I see him again.

During one of my visits, I asked, "Why are you always so happy?"

"I'm not always happy," he replied. "I have an inner joy that's linked to my relationship with God."

He gets his joy from God.

Many people confuse joy and happiness. Joy is a deep internal feeling of contentment that remains constant despite our circumstances. Happiness, however, is a fleeting emotion that is dependent on external circumstances.

The more grateful we are and the more we seek God and pursue a relationship with Him, the more joy will become our way of life. Happiness is momentary and fleeting. When the joy of the Lord becomes our strength, we can weather any storm knowing that He is with us wherever we go.

Let us receive the joy of the Lord, which is our strength. Let us stop embracing the happiness the world offers.

Prayer: Dear heavenly Father, thank You for being my exceeding joy. Thank You for the joy that is available to me just for being Your child. I glorify Your holy and matchless name. Please help me to always find joy in You, not the things of this world. Lord, I love You. Take full control of my life. In the mighty name of Jesus, amen.

For the word of God will never fail. (Luke 1:37, NLT)

...but I do this one thing: I forget about the things behind me and reach out for the things ahead of me. The goal I pursue is the prize of God's upward call in Christ Jesus. (Philippians 3:13–14, CEB)

I rejoice and celebrate in your faithful love because you saw my suffering—you were intimately acquainted with my deep distress. (Psalm 31:7, CEB)

I'm not saying these things just based on common sense, am I? Doesn't the Law itself say these things? (1 Corinthians 9:8, CEB)

We aren't like so many people who hustle the word of God to make a profit. We are speaking through Christ in the presence of God, as those who are sincere and as those who are sent from God. (2 Corinthians 2:17, CEB)

So now you are no longer strangers and aliens. Rather, you are fellow citizens with God's people, and you belong to God's household. (Ephesians 2:19, CEB)

My flesh and my heart may fail, but God is the strength of my heart and my portion forever. (Psalm 73:26)

For the Lord is good and his love endures forever; his faithfulness continues through all generations. (Psalm 100:5)

Our temporary minor problems are producing an eternal stockpile of glory for us that is beyond all comparison. We don't focus on the things that can be seen but on the things that can't be seen. The things that can be seen don't last, but the things that can't be seen are eternal. (2 Corinthians 4:17–18, CEB)

He entered the holy of holies once for all by his own blood, not by the blood of goats or calves, securing our deliverance for all time. (Hebrews 9:12, CEB)

Jesus Christ is the same yesterday, today, and forever! (Hebrews 13:8, CEB)

Then I acknowledged my sin to you and did not cover up my iniquity. I said, "I will confess my transgressions to the Lord." And you forgave the guilt of my sin. (Psalm 32:5)

Do not conform to the pattern of this world, but be transformed by the renewing of your mind. Then you will be able to test and approve what God's will is—his good, pleasing and perfect will. (Romans 12:2)

We demolish arguments and every pretension that sets itself up against the knowledge of God, and we take captive every thought to make it obedient to Christ. (2 Corinthians 10:5)

Those who live according to the flesh have their minds set on what the flesh desires; but those who live in accordance with the Spirit have their minds set on what the Spirit desires. The mind governed by the flesh is death, but the mind governed by the Spirit is life and peace. (Romans 8:5–6)

Finally, brothers and sisters, whatever is true, whatever is noble, whatever is right, whatever is pure, whatever is lovely, whatever is admirable—

if anything is excellent or praiseworthy—think about such things. (Philippians 4:8)

For the word of God is alive and active. Sharper than any double-edged sword, it penetrates even to dividing soul and spirit, joints and marrow; it judges the thoughts and attitudes of the heart. (Hebrews 4:12)

How precious to me are your thoughts, God! How vast is the sum of them! (Psalm 139:17)

You were taught, with regard to your former way of life, to put off your old self, which is being corrupted by its deceitful desires; to be made new in the attitude of your minds; and to put on the new self, created to be like God in true righteousness and holiness. (Ephesians 4:22–24)

Let the wicked forsake their ways and the unrighteous their thoughts. Let them turn to the Lord, and he will have mercy on them, and to our God, for he will freely pardon. "For my thoughts are not your thoughts, neither are your ways my ways," declares the Lord. (Isaiah 55:7–8)

What comes out of a person is what defiles them. For it is from within, out of a person's heart, that evil thoughts come—sexual immorality, theft, murder, adultery, greed, malice, deceit, lewdness, envy, slander, arrogance and folly. All these evils come from inside and defile a person. (Mark 7:20–23)

FINAL WORDS OF ENCOURAGEMENT
WENDI CHALLENGER

WE HOPE THE words in this book have provided comfort and hope. May they guide you, resonate with you, and remind you that every experience contributes to your story. You are not alone.

As you face each day, may God's grace be with you, and may the echoes of our shared faith offer a constant source of strength. We pray that you have found peace, courage, and enduring hope within these pages.

RESOURCES FOR FURTHER EXPLORATION

BOOKS

Jackie Hill Perry, *Jude: Contending for the Faith in Today's Culture* (Nashville, TN: B&H Books, 2020).

Jackie Hill Perry, *Upon Waking: 60 Meditations for Rest and Renewal* (Nashville, TN: B&H Books, 2023).

C.S. Lewis, *Mere Christianity* (London, UK: Geoffrey Bles, 1952).

Jonathan Cahn, *The Book of Mysteries* (Lake Mary, FL: Frontline, 2016).

Preston Perry, *How to Tell the Truth: The Story of How God Saved Me to Win Hearts, Not Just Arguments* (Carol Stream, IL: Tyndale Elevate, 2024).

Dr. Henry Cloud and Dr. John Townsend, *Boundaries: When to Say Yes, How to Say No to Take Control of Your Life* (Grand Rapids, MI: Zondervan, 2017).

Charles F. Stanley, *30 Life Principles* (Nashville, TN: Thomas Nelson, 2008).

(just to name a few)

MUSIC

"My Exceeding Joy," Londa Larmond.
"Never Lost," CeCe Winans.

"Made a Way," Travis Greene.

"I Smile," Kirk Franklin.

"Way Maker," Sinach (cover by Leeland).

"Lord You Are Good," Todd Galberth.

"Your Spirit," Tasha Cobbs Leonard, ft. Kierra Sheard.

"Intentional," Travis Greene.

"No Weapon," Fred Hammond.

"Make Room," Jonathan McReynolds.

"Trust in You," Lauren Daigle.

"In Christ Alone," Keith & Kristyn Getty.

"Thy Will," Hillary Scott & The Scott Family.

"I Will Follow," Chris Tomlin.

"Even If," MercyMe.

"What a Beautiful Name," Hillsong Worship.

"Jireh," Elevation Worship and Maverick City, ft. Chandler Moore & Naomi Raine.

"Great Is Your Mercy," Donnie McClurkin.

"I Feel Like Going On," Bishop Marvin Winans.

"Truth Be Told", Mathew West

(and so many more!)

You can find a variety of Bible reading plans for different interests on *YouVersion* and *BibleGateway*, as well as insightful online workshops from Tim Ross on the Tome app. Other valuable apps for ongoing inspiration and reflection include Our Daily Bread and Bible Inspirations—Daily. For podcasts, options to consider are *Bible U* (Dr. Darius Daniels), *The Dr. Cloud and*

Dr. Townsend Show (Dr. Henry Cloud and Dr. John Townsend), *In Totality* (Megan Ashley), and *With the Perrys*, to name a few. And finally, participate in events, workshops, and study groups hosted by local churches or your church to foster a sense of community and shared learning.